KNOSSOS

KNOSSOS

THE PALACE OF MINOS
A SURVEY OF THE MINOAN CIVILIZATION

MYTHOLOGY - ARCHAEOLOGY - HISTORY -
MUSEUM - EXCAVATIONS

SUPERVISION OF TEXTS
SOSSO LOGIADOU - PLATONOS

ARCHAEOLOGIST

ATHENS

COPYRIGHT: I. MATHIOULAKIS & Co
ADRESS: ANDROMEDAS 1 ATHENS 16231
TEL. 7661351 - 7227229
TRANSLATOR: DAVID HARDY

ISBN 960-7310-39-X

KNOSSOS

HISTORICAL INTRODUCTION

Crete appears to have been first inhabited during the Neolithic period — that is from the 6th millenium B.C. The earliest inhabitants may have come from Asia Minor. Their culture was still relatively primitive, but it had reached the stage of production, involving the cultivation of the soil and the keeping of domesticated animals. They knew how to make fine burnished pottery, frequently decorated with incised geometric motifs, and were capable of building stone houses, though they also still made use of caves for habitation. Metals were as yet unknown and the tools and weapons they needed (hammers, axes, knives etc.) were made of a range of hard stones, and obsidian from Melos. The simple, relatively primitive figurines suggest that they worshipped a female fertility goddess.

The Neolithic was followed by the Bronze Age civilisation which the English archaeologist **Arthur Evans,** who excavated the palace at knossos, called "Minoan" after **Minos,** the legendary king of Crete. This civilisation lasted over 1500 years, from 2600-1100 B.C., and reached the height of its prosperity in the 18th-16th centuries.

Very little was known about Minoan Crete before the great excavations of Greek and foreign archaeologists that began about 1900, and the discovery of the palaces of Knossos and Phaestos, with their astonishing architecture and wonderful finds. Its history had passed into the realm of legend and remained a distant memory in Greek tradition and mythology. The ancient authors speak mainly of Minos, the king who had his capital at Knossos, and was a wise lawgiver, a fair judge (who therefore judged souls in Hades after his death, along with Rhadamanthys and Aiakos) and a great sea-dominator. Homer calls him «companion of mighty Zeus", and Thucydides informs us that he was the first man to hold sway over the Aegean with his fleet, and that he captured and colonised the Cyklades, driving out the Carians, and freeing the seas from piracy. Plato speaks of the heavy tribute that the inhabitants of Attica were compelled to pay to Minos — the historical basis of the myth of Theseus can easily be recognised — and Aristotle attributes his thalassocracy to the geographical position of Crete.

Wonderful steatite rhyton in the shape of a bull's head. The horns were gilded, the eyes made of rock crystal and the muzzle of mother-of-pearl. Little palace at Knossos. 16th century B.C.

Types of Minoan Houses (Faience).

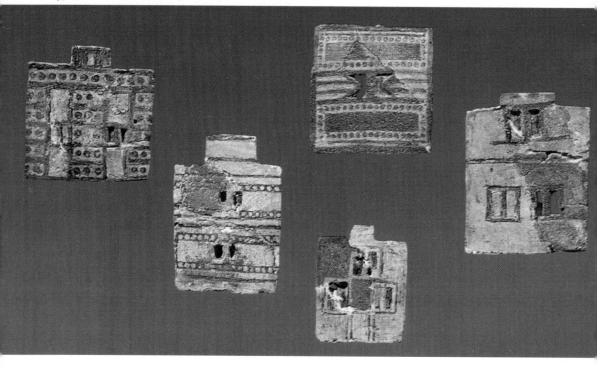

This position was, in fact, particularly favourable, both for the Minoan domination of the sea, and for the growth and development of their wonderful civilisation. It was the crossroads linking three continents, and the racial elements and cultural strands of Asia, Africa and Europe met and mingled here to produce a new way of life, a new philosophy of the world and an exceptionally fine art that still strikes one today with its freshness, charm, variety, and mobility.

The mixture of racial elements in Crete is demonstrated by the different skull-types discovered in the excavations there. In general terms, however, the Minoans form part of the so-called "Mediterranean type": they were of medium height and had black curly hair and

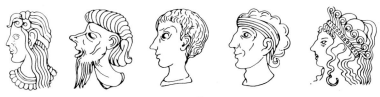

Minoan Types

brown eyes.Their language is not known, for the written texts have not yet been deciphered, but it appears to have belonged to a separate category of the Mediterranean languages. After 1450 B.C. when the Achaeans had established themselves in Crete, a very archaic form of Greek was used as the official language and gained some dissemination. This is the language that may be read in the Linear B texts deciphered by VENTRIS. The earlier Minoan language was still spoken alongside it by the Eteocretans ("the true Cretans"); this fact is attested by Eteocretan inscriptions discovered in East Crete, dating from the 6th and 5th centuries B.C.

Homer was aware that the inhabitants of Crete were divided into a number of tribes, and mentions the names of five of them: the Pelasgians, the Eteocretans, the Kydonians, the Achaeans and the Dorians, adding that each spoke its own language. He also emphasizes how densely populated Crete was, with its ninety cities, and mentions some of them, such as Knossos, Phaestos, Gortys, Lyttos, Kydonia, and Rhytion.

Excavation has demonstrated the truth of Homer's comments, revealing a host of Minoan sites, four of which were «palace» centres, developing around a large palace. Those known today, apart from Knossos and Phaestos, are at Malia and Zakros.

Evans divided the Minoan age chronologically, on the basis of the pottery, into "Early Minoan", "Middle Minoan" and "Late Minoan". Nowadays a different system of chronology has won general acceptance. It was proposed by Professor N. Platon, and is based upon the great destructions and the life of the Minoan palaces. It gives us the following periods for prehistoric Crete:

Neolithic period	(6000-2600 B.C.)
Minoan period	
Pre-palace period:	2600-1900 B.C.
First palace period:	1900-1700 B.C.
Second palace period:	1700-1350 B.C.
Post-palace period:	1350-1100 B.C.
Sub-Minoan period:	1100-1000 B.C.

The Pre-palace period (2600-1900 B.C.) With the arrival of new racial elements in Crete, bronze was used for the first time in the fabrication of tools and weapons. Its use quickly became widespread and continued to the end of the Minoan period. Not enough is known about the pre-palace settlements, but we do know that there were strongly built houses of stone and brick which had large numbers of rooms, pav ~ courtyards and, often, red plaster on the walls. The most typical of them were discovered at Vassiliki and Myrtos (Ierapetra). By way of contrast, the tombs of the period are very well known; there are large vaulted tombs (plain of the Messara), cist tombs cut rock inphelten (Mokhlos), chamber tombs (Agia Photia, Sitia) and grave compounds (Archanes, Khryssolakkos (Malia), Palaikastro, Zakros etc.) The wealth of finds in these tombs supplies us with information about the art and evolution of the pre-palace civilisation.

The pottery has a variety of main styles, known today by the names of Pyrgos, Ag. Onoufrios, Levina, Koumassa and Vassiliki. They are imitations of vessels made of straw, wood or hide and have incised, motifs full of movement painted and mottled decoration. Particularly fine examples are the Vassiliki style pots with their striking mottled decoration, produced by the firing, and their sophisticated shapes, like the "teapot" and the tall, beaked pitchers. The first polychrome pottery makes its appearance towards the end of the period.

In the field of miniature art, the gold ware is outstanding (jewellery from Mokhlos and the vaulted tombs of the Messara), as are the excellent, early examples of sealstones made of ivory and steatite.

Society seems to have been organised in genos, or 'clans', and farming, stock-raising, shipping and commerce were developed to a systematic level. The main forms of deity, and the most important cult symbols, had made their appearance in the sphere of religion, figurines of the Mother Goddess being typical.

At the beginning of the **First Palace period (1900-1700 B.C.)**, power began to be centred in the hands of kings, for some unknown reason, and the first large palace centres which had a wide cultural influence in the vital region around them, came into being.

Gold necklaces.

Small storage jar of the late period of the palace. Camaraic style. 18th century. Palace of Phaestos.

Strainer, decorated in dichrome floral style. From Zakro. Beginning of the 16th century B.C.

Camaraic vase of the late period with double axes. 18th century. Palace of Phaestos.

Bronze figurine of a worshipper, from Tylissos 16th century B.C.

Excavation has revealed four large palaces, at Knossos, Phaestos, Malia and Zakros, but there must have been others. It is clear from the scant remains of them that have been discovered beneath the later palaces that they possessed all the features of the fully developed Minoan architecture: the arrangement of the buildings around a central court, the fine façades of closely fitted blocks of poros stone, the large numbers of magazines, the sacred rooms, the different levels and storeys connected by small staircases, and the monumental entrances. The finest example is that uncovered in the west palace section at Phaestos. The most decorative style of pottery in the world was created in the palace workshops: the Kamares ware, named after the cave of Kamares where it was first discovered. Its motifs are polychrome and full of movement; they are mainly rosettes, spirals and hatching, painted on a shiny black background, and they are found on a variety of vase shapes, made with an astonishing technical perfection. The specialist workshops of the palaces also produced very fine vases or vessels of stone and faience; sealstones of precious or semi-precious stones, with hieroglyphics and dynamic scenes that are often naturalistic; solid elegant weapons and tools; vessels of bronze or silver; jewellery of marvelous technique (the "Pendant of the bees" from Chryssolakkos, Malia is famous) and

charming miniature sculpture.

Protopalatial terra-cottas are best known, however, from dedications in the Peak Sanctuaries (cult areas on the peaks of hills or mountains), which are typical of the period. The best known of those discovered so far come from Petsofa, Piskokefalo, Youktas, Kalo Khorio, Kofinas, Traostalos, and Vryssinas. The Minoan pantheon always has the mother goddess as its main element, and the use of sacred symbols (the sacred horns and the double axe) becomes general. Society was organised hierarchically, there was specialisation of labour and contacts with the outside world became more frequent. In the palace archives, use was made of the hieroglyphic script, which quickly developed into a linear one.

A terrible disaster, perhaps caused by earthquakes, reduced the first palace centres and the settlements of Crete to ruins, about 1700 B.C.

During the **Second Palace period (1700-1350 B.C.)**, Minoan civilisation reached its zenith. The new palaces that were built upon the ruins of the old ones were much more magnificent; the cities around them expanded and hummed with life; large numbers of rural villas, the residences of local governors, controlled great areas in the same way as the feudal towers of the Middle Ages; the roads increased in number and quality; the harbours were organized, and swift ships carried the products of farming and of Cretan art to the whole of the then civilized world, where they were exchanged for raw materials. The new palaces were multi-storeyed and invariably very complex. They had great courtyards, imposing or picturesque porticoes, broad easy staircases, processional paths and monumental entrances. The royal living quarters had tiers of doors (Polythyra), thrones and benches, as well as bathrooms and interior light wells, and there were rows of sacred quarters and magazines, crypts, and halls for audiences, banquet and sacred ceremonies Finally, there were ancillary areas of all kinds, including workshops, and a water-supply and drainage system based on very ingenuous principles. It is not surprising that buildings as large and complicated as this (the palace at Knossos covers 22.000 square metres and had over 1500 rooms) led the Greek imagination to create the myth of the labyrinth. The great palaces had one feature in common with the smaller ones, that were perhaps the summer residences of the kings (like those at Knossos, Archanes and Agia Triada near Phaestos): this was the won-

Excellent rhyton of rock crystal. The crystal ring at the base of the neck is decorated with gilded ivory. The beads on the handle are connected by a bronze wire. Palace at Zakros. 1500-1450 B.C.

Vase with a birds decoration. 1400 B.C. circa.
Post-minoan tombs. Katsamba - Heraklion.

derful fresco painting decorating the walls with fresh, lively scenes in an array of colours, or the dazzling white and veined blocks of gupsum that were used to cover the walls and floors.

The megara, or rural villas of the local governors, at Vathypetro, Sklavokambos, Tylissos, Metropolis (Gortys), Nirou Khani, Zou, Pyrgos (Myrtos), Praessos, Apano Zakros and elsewhere, had a farming and industrial character, emerging clearly from the interesting buildings that survive.

The social system was probably feudal and theocratic, and the king of each palace centre was also the supreme religious leader. There may have been a hierarchy of these priest-kings, headed by the ruler of Knossos. Thanks to this system, continuous peace — the famous **PAX MINOICA** — prevailed throughout the island, which facilitated the great cultural development, the charming, refined way of life, and the Cretan thalassocracy.

The art of the second palaces is naturalistie for the most part, and demonstrates the love of the Minoans for eternal, all-powerful and constantly renewed nature, as well as its internal, spiritual counter Part.

The Lily fresco, from the Villa of the lilies
at Amnissos.

18

The famous «Phaestos Disk». Both sides of the clay disk have hieroglyphic characters separately impressed by means of punches and arranged in a spiral. The script has not yet been deciphered. About 1600 B.C.

Wonderful ritual vase from the «Lustral Basin» at Zakros, unique for the marvellous use of the veins and spots in the polychrome marble, and for its bold shape. 1500-1450 B.C.

The famous «Rhyton of the Harvesters» from Ayia Triada. It is made of steatite and has scenes depicting a procession after the harvest and the winnowing. There is also a group of musicians singing, while the leader is holding a seistrum (rattle). 16th century B.C.

A variety of pottery styles developed: the marine style, with its lively motifs derived from the varied and striking world of the deep (octopuses, tritons, star-fishes, sea-snails, rocks, seaweed etc.); the floral style, with its fresh plants and open flowers; the decorated style, the basic motif of which is the spiral in a variety of complicated arrangements, though it also has sacred symbols and weapons; and, during the final phase of the period, the "palace" style, with its tectonic forms and decoration arranged in bands.

The fresco — a particular feature of the period — was used on a much greater scale than previously to decorate the palaces and wealthy houses. Landscapes were now depicted (royal gardens with exotic animals, such as monkeys, thickets of dense vegetation, birds, wild cats and deer), and there are scenes from cult and from social life: scenes of festival occasions in the palaces and sanctuaries (the miniature frescoes from Knossos,) of contests such as bull-leaping, held in honour of the deity, and of ritual, such as the "holy Communion" with the Parisienne. The relief fresco was used to portray majestic figures of princes and high priests (Prince with the Lilies) and sacred or imaginary animals (bulls, sphinxes, griffins etc.).

In the field of plastic art, the figures were more natural and complete, like the fifurines with the beautiful hairstyles from Piskokefalo (Sitia), and the plastic rhytons in the shapes of bulls or wild cats. The stone vases and vessels were made of fine veined, coloured stone or of rare, hard stones, alabaster, marble, rock crystal, obsidian, porphyry and basalt. They often take the form of sacred animals or animal heads, like the superb bulls' heads from Knossos and Zakros; or they may be decorated with masterful relief scenes like the ones from Agia Triada (harvesters rhyton, rhyton of the sacred games, cup of the report) and the rhyton with the peak sanctuary, from Zakros.

Faience was used for the working of rare, luxury items such as plastic rhytons (Zakros), decorative or votive plaques (the "town mosaic", and votive reliefs from Knossos), and unique figurines like the snake goddesses. There are works of a similar technical perfection in gold and ivory, such as the chrysselephantine bull-leaper from Knossos; royal gaming boards; gold rings engraved with miniature scenes of ritual, that afford so much information about Minoan religion; a wide range of jewellery; and vessels either made of gold or silver, or gilded. The handles of the long swords or elegant daggers of this period often have a gold covering and gold nails.

In addition to bronze weapons and tools of all kinds, many of which are like those of the present day, there are some very fine bronze vessels with carefully worked and graceful repoussée decoration.

The sealstones of the second palace period are made of precious and semi-precious stones, and represent wonderfully natural scenes from the animal world and from the religious cycle. They are usually lentoid or almond-shaped.

Archanes. Clay circular sanctuary of the godess with watching figures
on the roof. Early geometric era. 800 B.C.

The main deity is always the Mother Goddess, who is portrayed in her different forms. She is the chthonic goddess with the snakes, the "Ministress of the Animals" with lions and chamois, and the goddess of the heavens, with birds and stars. The powerful god of fertility was worshipped together with her, apparently in the form of a bull, as were the young couple, boy and girl, who died or were lost in the autumn and came back to the light and life in the spring, thus representing the cycle of nature. Alongside them there existed a whole exotic world of monstrous demons to serve them, and facilitate communications between man and the divinity.

The deities were worshipped in sanctuaries in the palaces, houses or countryside, in the peak sanctuaries and in sacred caves. Many of the features of Minoan religion passed into the cycle of Greek mystery religions. Most of the tombs were cut into the soft rock and had a square burial chamber and a sloping dromos. Some were still vaulted tombs with a circular or rectangular chamber.

The south royal tomb-sanctuary at Knossos consists of a complete building complex, with a small portico, a crypt with a sacred Pillar, a

The famous stone «Ayia Triada Sarcophagus» which has frescoes
portraying scenes of Minoan funeral ritual on all four sides.

A gold ring from Isopata with a representation of a dance of worship.

Famous gold jewel from Chryssolakkos, Malia. Two bees are sucking a drop of honey. Excellent example of Minoan gold work. About 1700 B.C.

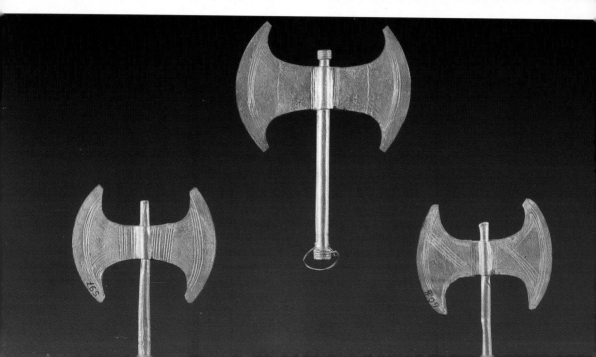

chamber cut into the rock, and an upper floor for the cult of the dead. It is very reminiscent of the "tomb of Minos" in Sicily described by Diodoros.

The hieroglyphic script of the preceding period now developed into Linear A. The surviving texts — there are about two hundred — are written in the unknown Minoan language on clay "tablets", and appear to contain information relating to accounts. They come from the archives of palaces or villas (Knossos, Archanes, Tylissos, Agia Triada, Phaestos, Zakros, Chania). The "Phaestos Disk", with its unique hieroglyphic text, belongs to the first phase of the second palace period. The hieroglyphic script seems to have survived from earlier times and to have been used by the priests to write religious texts.

About 1450, all the centres of the second palace period were destroyed by the terrible volcanic eruption of Santorini. Life was resumed only in the palace at Knossos, which was reconstructed and served as the residence of a new Achaean dynasty. The presence of this dynasty is attested both by the very archaic Greek language written in Linear B and by the appearance of the "Palace Style" pottery. Many changes were made in the arrangement of the palaces, and it is to this period that the "throne room" belongs, as does the final form and decoration (with frescoes) of the "Corridor of the Procession", and most of the other surviving frescoes.

Post-palace period (1350-1100 B.C.)

After the final destruction of about 1350, none of the Minoan palaces was re-inhabited. The Achaeans built their simple Mycenean megara on other sites, as yet unknown; remains of these have survived only over the ruins of earlier royal villas (as Agia Triada), and farms or houses (as Tylissos). Not even the palace of Idomeneus, the king of Knossos who took part in the Trojan War with his friend Meriones and 80 ships, has been discovered. A great number of Mycenean centres are known, however; these now spread throughout the whole of Crete, and most of them existed down into Greek times (Kydonia, Polýrrhenia, Kissamos, Knossos, Cortys, Phaestos, Lyktos, Arkadia, Rhytion etc.)

The basis of the new civilisation was Minoan, but its spirit was archaic Greek, and it showed a tendency towards an architectural structure and uniformity. The labyrinthine buildings were replaced by the austere Mycenean megaron; the predominant pottery style was the so-called "Mycenean koine", in which the same shapes were continually repeated, with simple decoration. and the frescoes lost their

Golden double axes from the Arcalochori cave.
16th century B.C.

former freedom and vigour. In the sphere of plastic clay art, there were large, impressive clay figurines, but even these were schematic and rigid (Metropolis (Gortys), Gournia, Gazi).

There was no substantial change in religion or cult. The tombs were mainly chamber tombs with a long dromos, as before, but the grave foods are poorer, and most of the jewels accompanying the dead were made of coloured glass paste.

The last phase of this period was a time of decline and disorder caused by the movement of the "Sea Peoples" in the East Mediterranean. The forerunners of the Dorians seem to have begun to arrive in Crete, for a number of new cultural features make their appearance in sporadic fashion: cremation of the dead, for example, iron weapons and tools, brooches - which attest a new style of dress - and geometric decorative motifs.

Crete entered upon the purely Greek period of its history with the arrival of massive waves of Dorians, about 1100 B.C. The **Protogeometric period** that followed **(1100-900 B.C.)** unfolded alongside the **Sub-Minoan,** for the earlier Cretan cultural tradition continued to offer resistance in certain areas, particularly the mountain centres of the Eteocretans in central and eastern Crete (Karfi (Lassithi), Vrokastro (Merambello), Praessos and other places near Sitia), and to exercise some influence on the uncouth conquerors. No one today doubts the contribution made by the Minoan and Mycenean civilisations to the creation of the Greek miracle.

The use of iron, and cremation of the dead became general, and the urns for the ashes are amongst the most characteristic vessels of the period. The finest examples of them come from Fortetsa, near Knossos, and some of them reveal the influence of Athens on the protogeometric art of Crete.

Reconstruction of the stepped portico (by Evans).

SIR ARTHUR EVANS
Ο ΔΗΜΟΣ ΗΡΑΚΛΕΙΟΥ
ΕΥΓΝΩΜΟΝΩΝ

HISTORY OF THE EXCAVATIONS
AT KNOSSOS

It had long been known that there had once existed a city called Knossos in this region, and indeed, the inhabitants often found ancient objects as they cultivated their fields.

The first man to excavate in the area was Minos Kalokairinos, a merchant of Heraklion, and a lover of antiquity. In·1878 he uncovered two of the palace store-rooms. The Turkish owners of the land compelled him to stop his investigations, and the attempts of Schliemann to purchase the "Kefala" hill came to nought because of the excessive sums they demanded. Fortune thus played a part in assisting Arthur Evans to begin systematic excavation in 1900, when the island had now been declared an independent State. He was at that time Director of the Ashmolean Museum in Oxford, and first visited Crete in order to study and decipher the unknown script that could be made out on sealstones.

The excavations began at a very rapid pace, and by the end of 1903 almost all of the palace had been uncovered and work began on the surrounding area. Evans continued his researches until 1931, with an interruption for the duration of the First World War. He subsequently published his work in four volumes entitled "The Palace of Minos at Knossos". His chief assistant was the archaeologist D. Mackenzie, who kept the basic day-book of the excavations.

From the beginning it proved necessary to preserve and restore the monuments that were being uncovered. A number of parts of the palace were restored in this way, and considerable use was made of reinforced cement in the work. The parts of the restoration that represent timber frames and other wooden structures were formerly painted yellow (the yellow colour has now been replaced by a colour conventionally representing the wood). In a number of places, moreover, copies were installed of the marvellous frescoes discovered during the excavation of the palace. This method of restoration has received much criticism, since it used materials foreign to Minoan architecture. Some scholars also dispute some of the conclusions of the pioneer English excavator.

All these questions aside, E v a n s is, constantly admired for his intuition, his creative imagination and his profound scholarship. It is basically to him that we owe the discovery of the marvellous Minoan world, which until his time was only dimly reflected in Greek Mythology. His services have brought him international fame and recognition.

As a mark of honour, therefore, and to perpetuate his memory, his bust has been erected on the south side of the west court of the palace.

After his death responsibility for the excavations at Knossos, which continue to the present day, was assumed by the British School of Archaeology.

KNOSSOS

TOUR AT THE PALACE

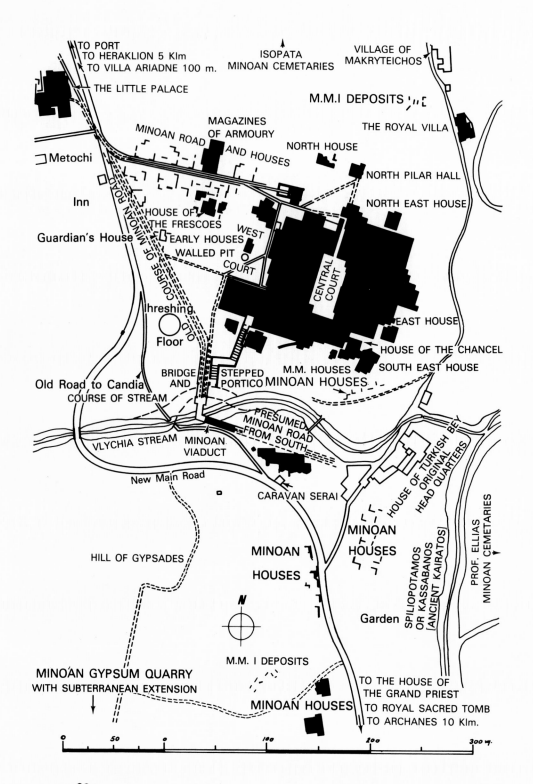

TO PORT
TO HERAKLION 5 Klm
TO VILLA ARIADNE 100 m.

ISOPATA
MINOAN CEMETARIES

VILLAGE OF
MAKRYTEICHOS

THE LITTLE PALACE

M.M.I DEPOSITS

MAGAZINES
OF ARMOURY
AND HOUSES

MINOAN ROAD

THE ROYAL VILLA

NORTH HOUSE

Metochi

NORTH PILAR HALL

NORTH EAST HOUSE

Inn

HOUSE OF
THE FRESCOES

WEST

Guardian's House

EARLY HOUSES

WALLED PIT

COURT

COURSE OF MINOAN ROAD

CENTRAL COURT

Ihreshing

Floor

OLD

EAST HOUSE

HOUSE OF THE CHANCEL

Old Road to Candia

BRIDGE
AND
COURSE OF STREAM

STEPPED
PORTICO

M.M. HOUSES

MINOAN HOUSES

SOUTH EAST HOUSE

PRESUMED
MINOAN ROAD
FROM SOUTH

VLYCHIA STREAM

MINOAN
VIADUCT

New Main Road

CARAVAN SERAI

HOUSE OF TURKISH BEY
ORIGINAL HEAD QUARTERS

HILL OF GYPSADES

MINOAN
HOUSES

MINOAN

HOUSES

SPILIOPOTAMOS
OR KASSABANOS
[ANCIENT KAIRATOS]

PROF. ELLIAS
MINOAN CEMETARIES

N

Garden

M.M. I DEPOSITS

MINOAN GYPSUM QUARRY
WITH SUBTERRANEAN EXTENSION

MINOAN HOUSES

TO THE HOUSE OF
THE GRAND PRIEST
TO ROYAL SACRED TOMB
TO ARCHANES 10 Klm.

0   50   0   100   200   300 ᵐ

KNOSSOS

TOUR AT THE PALACE OF KNOSSOS

The palace was the residence and headquarters of the king, the office-bearers and the priests, and although it was an administrative and economic centre, it also had a sacred character.

The palace is divided into two wings by the Central Court: the West wing **A** which housed the religious and official state rooms, and the East wing **B** where the domestic quarter and workshops were to be found.

WEST WING A

We enter the palace from the western approach, **A,** which is in the form of a ramp, and come first to the **paved west court I.** This is crossed by passages of slightly raised paved slabs, which are known as **processional ways,** because it is believed that the religious processions passed along them during the sacred ceremonies. One passage leads NE to the "Theatre", and a second to the South, to the palace.

In the West court there are **two altars 2** and three very large circular walled pits ('Kouloures'), which had been filled with the broken pottery used in the sacred rites **3.** At the bottom of the west and central pits, remains were found of houses dating from the end of the Prepalatial period. Houses of the Neopalatial period were excavated to the North of the pits, and tubular vases that had a religious function (the sacred snakes were kept in them) were discovered there. These may be seen in Heraklion Museum (room IV, case 46).

On the eastern side of the court rises the west façade of the palace, the lower courses of which consist of large gypsum blocks, blackened by the fire that destroyed the palace.

We enter the palace through the **West Porch 4,** a structure supported by a central column. Part of the base of this column, made of gypsum, survives in a good state of preservation (Minoan columns were made of wood, tapered from top to bottom, and stood on stone bases). The east wall of the Porch was decorated with a large fresco depicting a bullfight (only a part of the bull's foot is preserved). Two

West Facade of the Palace.

Circular depositories.

West Court.

Coloured relief of the «Prince with the Lilies» or «Priest-King».

rooms open to the South of this area: the small one served as a **Gate-keeper's lodge 5,** while the larger of the two, **6,** which may have held a throne, was used by the king to follow the rituals in the West court.

We now follow the **Corridor of the Procession 7,** which takes its name from the large fresco discovered here, depicting young men and women, almost life-size, bringing gifts to a female figure, who will have been a queen or a goddess. This corridor gives a good idea of the grandeur and luxury of the Minoan palaces: walls covered with multi-coloured frescoes, and a floor of white gypsum slabs, combined with smaller slabs of green schist, with red stucco in the joints between them. The corridor today comes to an abrupt end. In its original form it continued for about ten more paces to the SW corner (where the SW entrance was), turned left and ran along the whole length of the South side of the palace. At this point there was a terraced-portico. Underneath the corridor and the portico there were semi-basement rooms which are in a good state of preservation.

As we cannot today follow the Corridor of the Procession in order to enter the palace, we use the double door in the corner to our left, behind the large red column (restored area).

The small building that can be seen to the right, on a lower level, is the **South House 8.** It was built during the penultimate building phase, and may have belonged to the high priest of the palace.

The Corridor of the Procession had two passages leading to the main palace. One **9** is to the South and leads to the **Central Court 10.** The other takes one through the **South Propylaeum 11** to the first floor of the west wing of the palace. The SW part of the Propylaeum was restored by Evans. The walls were covered with frescoes, which

South-West columnes chamber and pillar crypt near the Propylaea.

Part of the South propulaea, with the sacred horns.

Part view of the palace at Knossos.

probably formed a continuation of the procession fresco, except that whereas the latter portrayed young women as well as men, this one has only young men. (In Minoan frescoes, the bodies of men are indicated by a satiated red colour and those of women by white. Men and women both have long hair and wear similar clothes and jewellery - bracelets on the arms, anklets on the legs and a sealstone on the wrist). The best preserved of the figures is the famous ''Cupbearer'', so called after the conical libation vase (rhyton) that he is holding. This youth typifies the ideal male figure of the period, with his slender waist, emphasized by the decorative metal belt. He is wearing a kilt which ends in a network, held in position by small weights of lead.

In the NE part of the Propylaeum can be seen a number of jars that were in fragments when they were discovered here and have since been reconstituted. They were undoubtedly placed here during the period of the ''re-occupation'' of the palace, when the Propylaeum was used as a store room.

To the North of the South Propylaeum there is a broad open **staircase 12** leading to the first floor, where the official rooms of the sanctuary **(piano nobile) 13** were located. From the top of the staircase there is a complete view of the surrounding area, with its row of hills, luxurious vegetation and the river Kairatos. Below, and slightly to the left, at the level of the Corridor of the Procession, we

43

Part of the South side of the palace at Knossos,
with the «sacred horns» and large pithoi.

can distinguish the sacred horns; according to one theory they originally stood on the south side of the palace roof.

The staircase flanked by colonnaded porticoes, the bases of which are the only parts preserved, leads to the entrance of the Sanctuary. Immediately after this there is an anteroom and a room identified by Evans as the **Tri-columnar Shrine 14**, depicted in frescoes. Of the shrine's three columns and three pillars, only a few of the bases are preserved. In the middle of this floor there was a corridor running the whole length of it; this corridor was parallel to the one on the ground floor that runs the length of the store rooms and can be seen below and to the West. These store-rooms are known as the **"West Magazines" 15,** and there were originally twenty-one of them; three of them fell into disuse during the Protopalatial period, however, and there are therefore only eighteen surviving today.

West Wing.

There are magazines in other parts of the palace, too, and the visitor may justifiably ask himself why there were so many storage areas. We must not forget that the king of Knossos, was a supreme secular and religious ruler. The magazines were therefore necessary in order to store the offerings to the deity, the taxes, the gifts and the revenue of the kingdom. The pithoi that can be seen today were used to hold oil and wine, and possibly also cereals, though few remains of the last have been found. The stone cists ("kaselles") in front of the pithoi may have contained precious vessels and vases; some of them certainly contained tools and weapons, as may be deduced from references in the tablets found here. There were other kaselles, finally, built below the floor of the **Corridor of the Magazines 16;** they were lined with sheets of lead, and were used to store liquids, or in some cases served as repositories. The west complex of the

Part of the west courtyard
and magazines.

The «Cup-bearer» from the procession
fresco (Heraklion Museum).

Restored Staircase to the second floor.

The ante-chamber of the Throne Room, with the lustral basin in the centre.

magazines, as Evans thinks, was contemporary with the first palace, from the 19th century, though it was also reused later, after the 17th century reconstruction. The magazines and corridor had neither windows nor light-wells, but were illuminated by oil lamps. The oil in the stores caught fire during the final destruction of the palace, and this caused the blackening on the walls. The stone pyramid-shaped bases that can be seen in the corridor were used to support large double axes.

Returning to the room of the "Tricolumnar Shrine", we come to the so called **"Great Hall" 17,** to the West of it, which has two columns in the middle of it. Two thirds of this room have been restored. It is, in fact, a particularly impressive area. Almost nothing has survived of the upper stories, either at Knossos or at the other Minoan palace structures, since, with the exception of the Grand Staircase on the

← *Southern house of the High Priest.*

52

east side, they were constructed of materials incapable of withstanding the frequent earthquakes.

From the northern edge of this floor we can see the difference in the thickness of the walls down on the ground floor. The first and the third are quite thin, while the second and fourth are thicker. This difference results directly from the need to support the colonnades of the upper quarters. To the North of the 'Great Hall' is the so called **"Room of the Sanctuary" 18,** which has six columns.

We proceed to the right to the **rooms 19** which have been restored on the basis of the plan of the ground floor walls. Copies of frescoes discovered at various points of the palace and now in the Heraklion Museum are displayed here. They fall into two groups, the purely decorative, with geometric compositions, and those depicting scenes from daily life, cult scenes and sacred rituals of the Minoans.

The east wall has the Toreador fresco. This was a contest or game involving young men and girls and a bull. It required exceptional dexterity and daring (they grasped the horns of the bull, executed a double somersault on its back and lept to the ground on

Upper hall of ceremonies of the western wing.

the other side) and frequently became dangerous. This contest, which was a particular favourite of the Minoans, should in no way be identified with the modern bull-fight, in which the aim is to overcome and kill the bull. Since the bull was a sacred animal, the contest might even be thought of as a ritual act,forming part of the total structure of religion. The fresco was discovered in the east wing of the palace.

To the left, on the north wall, may be seen the fresco of the 'Ladies in Blue', one of the first examples of Minoan painting. This was also discovered in the east wing.

To the left again, on the west wall, are displayed the two miniature frescoes, which were discovered in the throne room. Both of them depict festivals in the palace, in what one might call an impressionistic manner. The lower has a picture of women dancing in the sacred grove of Knossos. The spectators following it are the men on red. They are all greatly enjoying the spectacle and are raising their hands in applause. The upper fresco has a scene of a religious gathering in an outdoor area of the palace; this may be the central court, with the facade of the Columnar shrine in the centre.

There are two more frescoes beyond and to the left of the door, and a third exhibited opposite. All three were found in the "House of the Frescoes", and depict exotic gardens, with flowers and plants in a variety of colours, a blue bird and two blue monkeys. It is clear that the monkeys are tame from the ribbon around their heads and from their ability to carry out some task (in one fresco they are gathering papyrus reeds, and in the other plants that look like papyrus).

Finally, the small fresco of the Minoan officer leading black mercenaries also comes from the "House of the Frescoes".

We descend a spiral staircase, to the North of the rooms we are in, to the **Anteroom 20** of the Throne room on the ground floor. In the centre of this room, which opens into the Central Court, there is a porphyry bassin which Evans thought was used for ritual lustration (it was discovered nearby). There are stone benches to the right and left, and, during the excavations, carbonised remains of a wooden seat were discovered in the space between them on the north side; a wooden throne a copy of that in the next room has therefore been placed here . The Anteroom leads into the **"Throne Room" 21,** which name derives from the small gypsum throne that was preserved

Hall with copies of frescoes above
the throne-room.

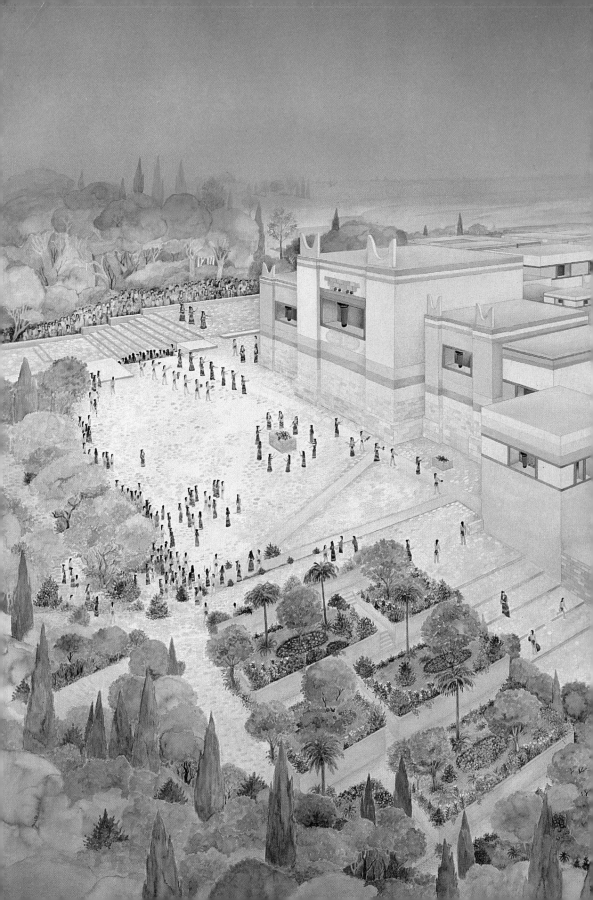

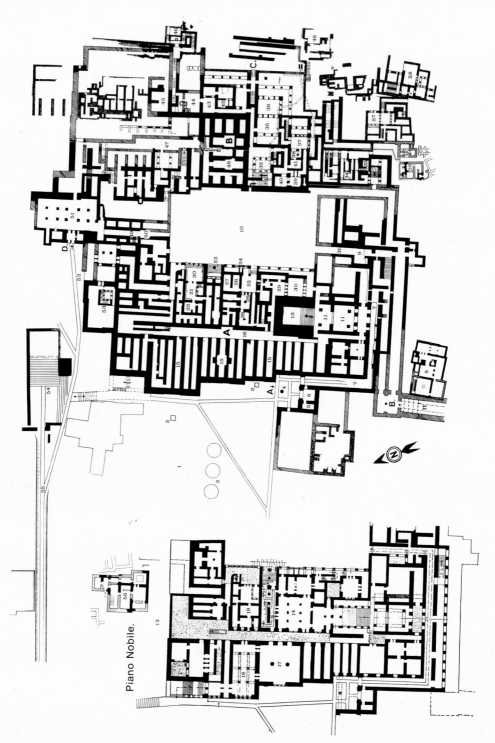

Piano Nobile.

58

PLAN OF THE PALACE OF MINOS AT KNOSSOS

A west wing.

A. West Entrance.
B. South Entrance.

B east wing.

C. East Entrance.
D. North Entrance.

1. West Court.
2. Altars.
3. Sacred Waste Pits, ('Koulouras').
4. West Porch.
5. Gate-keeper's Lodge.
6. Room with Throne.
7. Corridor of the Procession.
8. South House.
9. Corridor to the Central Court.
10. Central Court.
11. South Propylaeum.
12. Staircase.
13. Piano Nobile.
14. Tri-Columnar Shrine.
15. West Magazines.
16. Corridor of the Magazines.
17. Great Hall.
18. Room of the Shrine.
19. Rooms with copies of frescoes.
20. Anteroom to the Throne Room.

21. Throne Room.
22. Interior Shrine.
23. Central Staircase.
24. Tri-partite Shrine.
25. Anteroom of the Pillar Crypts.
26. Room of the Tall Pithos.
27. Temple Repositories.
28. Square-Pillar Crypts.
29. Area of the "Chariot Tablets".
30. "Temple of Rhea".
31. The Prince with the Lilies.
32. Grand Staircase.
33. Shrine of the Double Axes.
34. Lustral Basin.
35. Hall of the Double Axes or
36. King's Megaron.
37. Queen's Megaron.
38. Queen's Bathroom.
39. Queen's Toilet Room.
40. Court of the Distaffs.

41. Treasury.
42. Lapidary's Workshop.
43. Potter's Workshop.
44. Court of the Stone Spout.
45. Magazines of the Giant Pithoi.
46. East Bastion.
47. Corridor of the Draught Board.
48. Magazine of the Pithoi with Medallions.
49. Bastion of the N. Entrance.
50. Passage of the N. Entrance.
51. Custom House.
52. NW Entrance.
53. Lustral Basin.
54. Theatre.
55. Royal Road.
56. House of the Frescoes.
57. House of the Chancel Screen.
58. SE House.
59. House of the Sacrified Oxen.
60. House of the Fallen Blocks.

The «Ladies in Blue», a fresco with a blue background.

intact in the position it still occupies today,[1] as were the stone benches. The room very probably had a religious function, the priest-king sitting on the throne, with the priests on either side on the benches. The sacred nature of the area is also idicated by the lustral basin opposite (this is clearly not a bath, since it has no drain). The purification ritual will have been symbolic: those involved descended the small flight of steps, thus coming closer to mother earth, and there were their bodies sprinkled with holy water. A photograph is particularly important, since it shows a number of loaf-shaped alabaster vases on the floor, and a broken pithos in the corner. It is thought that at the time the palace was destroyed, a ritual was taking place in this area to appease the divinities, and that it was abruptly broken off, so that these vessels were left in position.

The north and west walls of the room were decorated with a large fresco representing griffins amongst reed-like vegetation, that may be seen in the restored copies. The griffin is thought to have

[1] The President of the International Court at the Hague has a seat that is a copy of this throne, since Minos was thought to be the first judge in the world.

The famous «Bull-leaping» fresco.

symbolised the three forms of the deity: the heavenly, with its eagle's head, the earthly, with its lion's body, and the subterranean, with its tail in the form of a snake.

Further inside this room there was a small **niche 22** on a podium. According to Evans the priest-king withdrew into the inner area to fast and meditate. The area, which was dark, was lit by a stone lamp.

We emerge onto the **Central Court,** one of the most characteristic features of Minoan palace architecture. The different parts of the palace were built around it, and it is probable that ritual ceremonies were held here, so that a large audience could follow them. In the corner of the court we can see, as we come out of the Throne room, part of the drainage system. Stone drains lead the rain water to a central sewer.

The Central Court was paved, but very few traces of the paving have been preserved. Proceeding South from the Throne room, we come to the **Central Staircase 23,** of which only four steps are preserved today. It originally had two flights, and on the lower, broader one, there were large columns supporting the roof, the bases of which can still be seen amidst the steps.

To the left, next to the Central Staircase, is the facade of the

Tripartite Shrine 24. Traces of the circular column bases can be made out on the stylobate. The middle was higher than the rest, and supported a central column. There were sacred horns between the columns and on the entablature. To the South, there are some steps leading to an anteroom with a stone seat, where the traces of the fire that finally destroyed the palace can clearly be distinguished. We now move on to the **Shrine of the Pillar Crypts 25.** The first room, to the right of the anteroom is known as **"The Room of the Tall Pithos" 26.** Here we see one of the finest pithoi from the first neopalatial phase; it was discovered intact and remains **in situ.** Next door, to the left, are the **"Temple Repositories" 27.** These two large storage-chests, built below the floor, were made of poros stone and were provided with sheets of lead, against damp. In them were found the most famous of the Minoan figurines, the "Snake Goddesses". The chests were covered in at a later date and three smaller ones built on top of them.

To the west of the Ante-room of the Crypts are the **Square-Pillar Crypts 28.** The Double Axe has been incised a large number of times on each pillar. There are rectangular stone basins near each column, for offerings of animal sacrifices. One of the rooms to the right was used as a store-room, and in the other is preserved a low ledge with vats. To the South of the ante-room is the area of the **Chariot tablets 29,** and still further to the South, an area occupied by a temple of Greek times (Temple of Rhea) **30;** in the room contiguous with it there is a clay bath tub, in which Linear B tablets were found.

We now return to the Central Court. The end of the Corridor of the Procession may be seen on the south side. As we have seen, this corridor ran the whole length of the south side of the palace, turned left again, and came out onto the Central Court.

The remains of one of the most famous frescoes, the **Priest-king, or Prince with the Lilies 31** were found in pieces on the floor somewhere in this area.

The youth, in low relief, is wearing a crown of lilies and peacock feathers, a gold necklace with beads in the form of lilies, and a simple kilt, secured by a broad belt. He may have been leading the sacred griffin or a sphinx on a rope. The scene is greatly restored, very few pieces of the original being preserved (part of the feathers of the crest, the chest, the two legs and the arm of the prince).

Below, in the middle of the south side of the palace was the **South Entrance B.**

← *The famous alabaster throne of Minos, the priest-King. It is framed by griffins, which were imaginary sacred animals.*

North Entrance Passage.
(After Evans).

The «Central Staircase» in the W. wing
of the palace at Knossos.

The larger «Snake Goddess»,
a faience figurine.

The smallest «Snake Goddess»,
a faience figurine.

The famous «Parisienne», a priestess of the deity.
From a fresco at Knossos, 15th century B.C.

69

The "King - Priest" or "Prince" (copy).

East Wing.

← View from the eastern wing to the sanctuaries
of the central courtyard.

74

EAST WING B

Whereas the West wing opposite had only two stories in addition to the ground floor on the level of the Central Court, the East wing had four stories as well as a ground floor. Communication between them was by the **Grand Staircase 32,** one of the best preserved parts of the palace. From the landing we can see the first floor, which has been restored, almost on a level with the Court. From this point to the ground floor, there are four surviving flights of stairs, the first two of which are restored, while the lower two are preserved just as they were found. There are also traces of a fifth flight. This staircase formed the official approach to the royal quarters, though there were also auxiliary staircases for daily use.

The walls of the landings of the staircase were covered with fresco paintings; a copy of one of these may be seen on the east wall of the adjoining verandah depicting shields on a frieze of spiral. There are no shields surviving from this period, for they were made of ox-hide (the shape of them is known from small specimens in ivory or other materials, and also from the descriptions in Homer's Iliad). In the Iliad they are described as "seven-oxhide shields" — that is of seven skins sewn one on top of the other.

We pass through a door in the south side of the landing, through a crooked corridor and some other apartments and come to a room with a bath. Amongst the pottery found hereby were a few vases decorated with white lilies. Further it can be seen part of the drainage system, with stone conduits. To the South of it is the "**Shrine of the Double Axes**" **33,** which is today covered over.

Two pairs of sacred horns still stand on a pedestal on the north side, and next to them are clay figurines of a goddess and worshippers. The shrine belongs to the post-palace period. A short way to the South there is a **Lustral Basin 34,** similar to the one in the Throne room.

Returning to the landing with the shields, we descend the Grand Staircase to the ground floor. We now get a better view, from the small colonnade running alongside the area of the central light-well system that supplies light vertically to all the floors. A system of light-wells was generally used in the residential quarters of all the Minoan palaces. It supplies light and air indirectly to each successive floor, and mitigates the summer heat, while also protecting the rooms from the cold of winter.

The gypsum slabs of the colonnades and of the East-West corridor adjoining it, are in a very good state of preservation. At the beginning of the corridor there is a small doorway and it is possible to see how the door operated from the traces remaining on the threshold. The hinge and the rub marks show that the wooden door opened to the right.

From the corridor we enter the **Hall of the Double Axes 35,** or the **King's Megaron 36** to the right. The two sections of which it consists communicate with each other through a tier of doorways, which continues through to the colonnade of the light well in the east. The

Great stairway and veranda
of the shields.

Grand Staircase of the East Wing:
The Hall of the Colonnades.

King's Megaron and Stoa.

two light-wells at the sides of the room are based on a vertical system of natural ventilation, which achieves a regular circulation of air between them. At the ground level of the light well we can distinguish part of the circuit drainage system. The ashlar stones of the west light well have the sacred double axe which gave the room its name, incised on them in a number of places. The quarter towards the East light well was probably used for audiences with the king, for remains of a throne were found here. On the gypsum, which has been calcinated by fire, it is possible to make out traces of the canopy that covered the throne supported on columns.

The east section of the Hall is one of the grandest parts of the palace, with the triple tier of doorways that closed it in on three sides and with its external angular colonnade.

In Minoan times, large figure of eight shields of ox-hide hung on the north wall, where Evans placed a wooden throne.

Passing through a small door in the South of the Hall of the Double Axes, we proceed along a crooked corridor and come to the **Queen's Megaron 37,** a room smaller than that of the king, but equally imposing with its two light-wells. This room communicates with the east light well by means of two columns, the bases of which

are in a good state of preservation today. Some parts of the floor have been removed, to reveal earlier paved surfaces, constructed at different periods and in different ways. The lowest is made of rough stones, the middle one of slabs in mosaic, and the uppermost of finely worked gypsum slabs. The fresco on the east wall, with the dolphins, fish and sea-urchins, belongs to neopalatial periods; during the last, it was covered by another with a frieze of spirals. Another fresco in this room, on a post of the east partition, shows a girl dancing, with her hair blowing in the wind as she turns. Her dress is particularly interesting, with its short-sleeved bolero, decorated with coloured embroidery (the original fresco is in Heraklion Museum).

To the west is the **Queen's Bathroom 38.** The bath, which was restored from fragments, is, like all the others, a small sitting bath. Both the walls of the small corridor through which we passed, and the lower parts of the walls of the bathroom were faced with tall gypsum slabs; the upper part of the walls was covered with monochrome frescoes, transversed by decorative friezes. The small wall painting here is the original, but the colours are not very well preserved. The column in the bathroom was restored in accordance with the traces preserved on the base of it. According to Evans, traces of three columns of the same style were found during the excavation of the Little Palace. They are reminiscent of Egyptian models, with capitals imitating lotus in blossoms.

Going through the small door in the South of the bathroom and along the corridor beyond it, we come to the **Queen's Toilet Room 39.** The door and window of this room open on to a light well which is called the **Court of the Distaffs 40,** since the symbol of the distaff is incised on the wall. The low ledge along the south wall was used to hold the utensils for the toilet. Above this point there was a cistern and two conduits built into the wall, which carried the rainwater and the waste from the toilets on the floor above into the drains of the toilet next door, in the small room to the east. There is a groove in the partitions of this room, on the right-hand gypsum plaque, and the carbonised remains found during the excavation indicate that this is where the wooden seat was supported. The area was screened off by gypsum partitions on either side. The drainage system can be seen very clearly from the door. All the water from the light wells, and the bathrooms and toilets ultimately found its way into the central drain which flowed into the river Kairatos.

Queen's Bathroom.

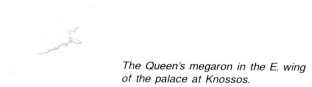

The Queen's megaron in the E. wing of the palace at Knossos.

Remains of precious objects were found in the small room with the wooden door, on the right, at the beginning of the corridor **(Treasury) 41.** As we proceed along this half-lit corridor, we can make out the lower part of a small stone staircase and its "sotto scala": here was found a group of miniature figurines in ivory and gold, belonging to a group of bull-fighting.

Continuing along the same corridor we come back to the ground floor level of the great staircase, at the point from which we started — an indication of the labyrinthine nature of the palace. We now proceed to cross the corridor in front of the Hall of the double axes, and come to the workshops area. On the walls to the right and left we can see the sockets for the vertical and horizontal beams that were put here to resist earthquake shocks. The traces of the fire here are quite clear.

A little further on we can see the **Lapidary's Workshop 42.** Here basalt was worked; this is a greenish or reddish stone with yellow crystals that was imported from the area of Taygetos in the Peloponnese. The work on some of the stones was left half-finished: sawn and polished, they remained in their original position because of the sudden nature of the destruction.

Immediately after that we come to a small room known as the **Potter's Workshop 43,** and beyond this to the **Court of the Stone Spout 44,** from which a long stone conduit drained off the rain water into a blind well, today covered with an iron grille.

Opposite are the **Magazines of the Giant Pithoi 45.** These jars are the largest so far discovered, and date from the Protopalatial period.

Descending the staircase in front of us, which was restored by Evans, we now come to the **East Bastion 46** of **East Entrance C.** According to Evans, the area in which the bull-leaping took place lay beyond this point. Here we can see yet another sort of the drainage system. The rain water was conducted down a steep incline from the upper levels to the ground floor. The water would have picked up great speed as it flowed, however, and would have spilled out of the channel at the bends; to prevent this, an exceendingly clever system was adopted: the channel at the side of the staircase followed a parabolic curve, which checks the speed of the water so that its impetus is not so great when it gets to the corners. On the landings of the staircase there are two stone troughs to filter the water.

Returning in front of the Magazines of the Giant Pithoi, and continuing our ascent up the same staircase, we come to the

Fresco of the danser at the Queen's apartments. 15th century B.C.

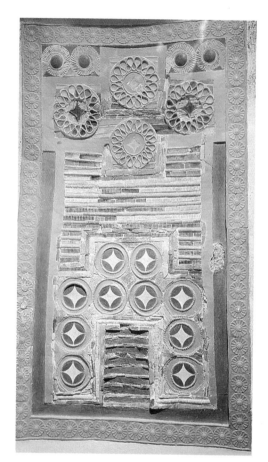

The «zatrichion» (chess), royal game. Palace of Knossos. 16th B.C.

Drainage pipes from the store rooms and laboratories of the east wing.

Pithoi with relief medallions.

← View to the bastion of the bull of the northern entrance and to the NW entrance.

90

Corridor of the Draught Board 47, which took its name from the royal gaming board (for playing) found here. It is made of ivory, rock crystal, gold, lapis lazuli and faience. The pawns were conical in shape and made of ivory. The whole is on exhibition in room IV of Heraklion Museum (case 57).

Near the point where the gaming board was found we can see the system that supplied drinking water, beneath an iron grille. The clay pipes have a ring fitting, and consist of cylinders tapered towards one end, so as to produce a greater head of water; this prevents the system from blocking up by washing away the various salts and not allowing them to adhere to the inside of the pipes.

Drinking water came from Mount Jouktas to the South of the palace. There are thus three different water and drainage systems in the palace: one for drinking water, one for rainwater and a third to carry away the sewage.

To the west can be seen the **Magazine of the Pithoi with the Medallions 48** with rosettes enclosed within the medallions in relief.

We now proceed to the **North Entrance D.** This is the only part of the palace that has a controlling defence system. Fortifications are unknown in Minoan architecture, on account of the **Pax Minoica.** The passage was originally wider, but was later narrowed, probably to achieve securer defence. **The west 49** of the two bastions that controlled the entrance has been restored, and a copy of the fresco depicting the hunting of a wild bull has been placed here. There is an olive tree in low relief next to the animal, which is weary and panting as a result of the chase. The way in which these animals were caught is known from the scenes on the two gold cups found in the tomb at Vaphio near Sparta.

We descend to the northern entrance by the **Sloping Passage 50** below which runs the central drainage conduit. On the stone block at the side of it are incised mason's symbols, such as the trident, the double axe, and the star. The corridor ends to the North in a large room (the **"Custom House"** of Evans) **51,** with two columns and eight gypsum pillars.

To the left, and on a higher level is the **Northwest entrance 52** to the palace. Unlike the North entrance, which was the main one leading from the road coming from the harbour to the palace, this entrance probably had a religious character since it is flanked by a **Lustral basin 53.** There the visitor to the sanctuary, or anyone who was about to take part in the religious ceremonies, had to undergo lustration.

Proceeding to the West we come to the **Theatre 54,** an area which was connected with religious ritual, as can be seen from the miniature frescoes in the palace. It is believed that the royal box was on the raised podium, at the point where the tiers of seats meet, while the spectators sat on the steps of the tiers. "The Theatral area" was in the middle.

Two paved causeways (one to the South crossing the seats, and one in the centre) meet just below at the **"Royal Road" 55** — the oldest in Europe, dating from the period of the first palace. The paving is in a relatively good state of preservation, as are the gutters for rain-water on either side. There were a variety of buildings on both sides of this road, such as the **"House of the Frescoes" 56** and

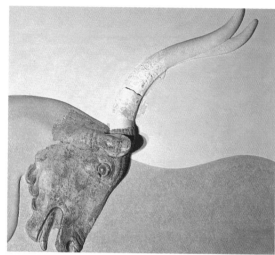

The relief fresco of the charging bull of the North Entrance. (Heraklion Museum).

the "**Armoury**". The Royal Road leads to the **Little palace,** on the other side of the modern road from Knossos to Heraklion.

In concluding our tour, we should note that only a few houses of the city around the palace have been excavated, and most of these were the residences of noble, wealthy Minoans.

Very close to the palace, on the south east side, are the remains of the "**House of the Chancel Screen**" **57,** the "**SE House**" **58,** the "**House of the Sacrificed Oxen**"**59,** the "**House of the Fallen Blocks**" **60,** and the "**House of the Monolithic Pillars**". It is worth visiting the Minoan Inn **(Caravanserai)** to the South, and the "**Southern Royal Tomb**" to the South of that and on the right of the road from Knossos to Spilia; this is a two-storied building with a burial chamber and a pillar crypt; also worth visiting is the "**Royal Villa**" to the NE of the palace and the "**Little Palace**". To the West of the Little Palace is the "**Villa Ariadne**", built by Evans in 1907 and used as a residence and for study purposes by himself and his colleagues.

The city's cemeteries stretched in almost every direction (on the sites of Sopata, Ayios Ioannis, Zafer-Papoura, Sanatorio, Gypsades, Monastiriako Kefali and Profitis Ilias), and the tombs in them have yielded many rich and valuable finds.

The visitor should bear in mind that to tour the Palace fully requires approximately two hours.

NW entrance and lustral basin.

The theatre of Knossos from the west.

Royal Villa of Knossos. At the left,
the sacred tribune. In the background,
the entrance to the crypt.

The Royal Road.

Corridor, courtyard, entrance of the $\longrightarrow$
southern royal tomb of Knossos.
16th century B.C.